Praise for *under the influence* . . .

"Reading *under the influence* is like stumbling upon a photograph album that spans six decades. Each sequential "photo" embodies the particular forces that have shaped the poet's consciousness, concerns, and style. The musicality, oral tradition of story telling, and inventiveness of language found in *Portrait of the Artist as a Young Man* comes to mind but cat holds her reader closer."
— Betsy Warland, *Oscar of Between — A Memoir of Identity and Ideas*

"cat mac's *Under the Influence* asks n shows sew much
- ar past refrains admonishyuns
shaping punishing echoes that
prevent us from living fullee in th
present or with attensyun n care
n breething courage a chorus from
wher wev escaped in2 th lite love
n lafftr uv th reel present living
- its a book uv writing that is uneek
and wundrful ovrlays threddings
layrs n voices remonstrating
n fritening memoreez n th amayzing
possibiliteez uv living free uv thos
limiting ghosts in2 th present
unhamperd touch - brillyant writing"
— bill bissett, *hungree throat*

under the influence

cat mac

under the influence

GusGus Press • Bedazzled Ink Publishing
Fairfield, California

978-1-943837-42-7 paperback

Cover Art
by
Lori Kenney

Cover Design
by

DESIGNS

GusGus Press
a division of
Bedazzled Ink Publishing, LLC
Fairfield, California
http://www.bedazzledink.com

to my parents
alex and maureen
who instilled within me a kernel of hope
without which i may never have made it

Contents

bloodline

gathering

activity behind the retina. raw nerve. ending. poet manque. supertense. pixilate. nerve. us. ever-to-be-suppressed. break. down. cloaked in echoes. indelible dictum *she bears witness to "take me home/suite: home and leave me there" blankbody springs off to off spring to, atomic arms of non-chaos/ the infancy house where she's caught interstices/interspaces being other than herself, she intones and sings a soft-core-west-end-hymn, blind in the amorphous watery, before clouds and slipping into the other half, as doppelgängers hover ever-present, her life borders on being double, babies perception within touching distance of the body proper but she does not want to be touched in the louche dark room where the trajectory of her movements fructify, wax, wane, wend her way. she never knew herself, passes, turns, but can remember the demands and is struck by where within her, wherewithal, what it is to be a subtle body, a some body? she wanders, clamps her feelings into place, invents a would-be self that summons affection, stretches phantom limbs and grow-young-atmospheric-muscle-tone. she returns to herself, instant bodily replay, the textsoul guided and falling into the body needs a buddy, changes this changeling who hears the underside of foretaste, cold in the shadow but bodying forth, incisive, bone of bone. divisive. flesh of flesh. split. into lacuna. open. roots. sets foot. the sound skin makes. queen/size iron cry. déjà palpe. dissipating into the velocity. this mortal coil.*

climbing cate's ladder. a cloud in address. the place of saying:

the daughter of the girl

my mother would open the grade two door
pick up the credit union books on the ledge

john bates would say

    "is that your mom? is she ever pretty"

i was in love with her
   glamorous   a liz taylor
     hair platimum in a beehive
perfect liner around her gentle
          eyes
     the hazel of
   moss   cedar/soft

at eight i'd float on my back in halfmoon bay
 her tender hand
   open   beneath my spine
   taken up by the water and the belief she had in me
    stead/fast

her hand would be
        there
      would be
warm cookies on the kitchen table
       there
     she was
  catechism   guides   piano   soccer

she has only one picture of herself as a child   selling valentines
                          she was not smiling

her aunt cut it out of The Province
                              she loved her father
                    who threw her zootsuit into the fire
                    used her new coat as a mat
                              (she forgot to hang it up)
beat her mother 'til she pulled him off

my mother had to wear cheap Woolworth's skirts
her mother would buy five the same when they were on sale

she became the only girl in Vancouver with a paper route
                    bought herself one good skirt (
                    when she dyed her hair at fifteen
                         her mother cut it off

she drives fast hot cars
my mother wears red   and black   and heels

she had three kids in diapers at the same time
a fourth kid (autistic)

the son of the boy

born older than his father

> gray eyes
> lanky frame
> large feet

he puts kittens in a basket   hangs it up on the clothesline
yanks up and
      down
            his little sister cries

sees his other sister kissing her sweetheart outside his bedroom window
shoots the light out with a shotgun

my father, Sisyphus

walks from Yale Street to the top of Grouse Mountain with skis on his back
for five minutes of going down

falls twelve floors from a West End highrise washing windows
only breaks his ankles

my father plays accordian by ear
recites *The Shooting of Dan McGrew* by heart

grows beets and butter lettuce between petunias and impatiens keeps a
teddy bear
          in the crook of the lilac tree

he smokes salmon in the backyard
hangs geese from the clothesline
dumps a dead moose on our lawn
he shoves a bottle of vodka under the seat of his ford pickup

takes us to the local park
        where we fry bacon and eggs
              toast bread on branches

tells me and Sal he's leaving

                                        we stand at the front door crying
                                        pull on the sleeve of his jacket

he takes the guns out of his truck
                              hangs them back on the wall

my father looked after his father
at twelve he asked his Dad
                              not to cheat at cards
                              not to sell cars that were lemons
and not
                     to touch the kids at school

suite to their bedroom

there was a crooked man and he had a crooked house.
he had a crooked little father.

papa was a rollin' stone. whatever he did. we couldn't have known. and when he
died. left me cold as stone

i forget the first bedroom. Adderley St. glow-in-the-dark marys and josephs,
a crib for molly. wee three in the attic.

i cannot forget the second. 1960's purple plush. faded wooden crucifix over
their bed. high heels sleeping 'mongst clumps o' dust.

i loved my mother's side of the bed. falling into the feathery soft. smell of
her scalp. "your dad's going hunting. who wants to sleep with your ol' mom
tonight?" everyone loved to. but

papa was a rollin' stone. whatever he did. we couldn't have known. and when he
died. i cried "leave me alone"

inside the self-same walls. i saw my father cry only once. the day his father
died. we knelt around the bed. eyes closed. heads bowed. hands crossed.
rosary beads draping mother's palm, listening to our father. sob

holy mary. mother of god. pray for us sinners.

halfmoon bay

my grandmother cannot swim
today she lays her glasses near the ocean's edge
inches into the cool, blue oyster pool
pats the waves with palms and laughs

she creeps in toes first   genuflects
her white knees christened
shouts in gaelic "och och" at the cold
ambersoft kelp brush her thighs
breathe like fingers that tickle the few hairs outside her suit

she turns

algae lipping
rolls her finger round her tongue
          soft   wet
sinks her plump form of scones and oatcakes onto the gritty ledge
smiles at the sunhats on the porch

handhold

my grandmother's hands
          are folded aptly
                    around *Alias Grace*
and *The Selkirk Settlers*
            which i return to her
                      as i had promised
as if enough
        wasn't already squeezed
                  into Christmas Day

her fingernails
        are buffed clairol pink
                      her treasured weekly ritual
of human contact

she lines the books up
            corner to corner
                    (some semblance of order)
heaves her hunched form
          upright in the wheelchair
                        presses a smile
into the lens

on the table beside her
          a scotch
                that she cannot reach

soon Grammo will be whisked away
                  the gift
                        i carefully made for her
will be hurled
        into a bag
              of unopened gifts

my grandmother
        can no longer hold things:

o how i long
        to hold the hands
                that hold the books
        to hold the woman
                that holds my hands

but i stall
        at the thought as if my grandfather's touch
spilled from hers

a suite to call answer

i.

a practice one generation removed

grandfather jumps from the top of the Hotel Vancouver

                                        like flames

i know this war

mines deeper than blood

                        cells occupied.

no brief flitting of a family
                    marching

                    (whose dead body lays at the side of the road?)

ii.

eyes blending into the head

                    if i could straighten out these eyes

                        my skin

iii.

these legs are little
                          but they will get me there

standstill
                    two ducks cross Burrard Street Bridge

drivers lean on steering wheels struck dumb

                                              this worldliness

iv.

sometimes there is just too much beauty

i'm grateful for hands stroking this leaf
                                          furrysoft as a cat's ear
                        feathers posing as leaves

tissue blows from crow's nose
the garden is growing with us

                        our heatherhappywearyhearts

                                        on mossy spots
                                                      rocks

die ungelhaltene

i.

make your mother sigh

baby

so cry to the wynd
three sheets   and a limb

the pain
in sin

       (cere)

lays at her trunk   arms axed

                                 outside

the holy tree trembles into terre-verte

                                       displaced, she casts

stellar flakes to gods

blind
in the eye

ii.

the unheld

first touch

no one hears

her treble O

pick those eyes up off the ground and put them in their sockets
leave them there

on the border
land

        the glass
                house

leaf against pane and brick

            howl   howl

she pulls the counterpane up around her ears
wears her clothes to bed

lifeline

a heartbreak kid

i.

she dreams of leaky condo(m)s
of uteruslessness and the mortgager
(beside mortician in Rogets)

why is she singing this?
she's crawled back(words) inside the guava sky
abated by her own
interior drama

a nervous child haunted
by the habit of peeing every ten minutes
"Shame on you" her nanny rasps and her mother before her . . .
"It's psychogenic" the psychologist pronounces
"Make her hold it."

ii.

polyanna made angel visits
the bad girl, chick of her will
dragged heavy sexual baggage into all-canadian households
where they tsk-tsked

didn't know what was worse
wasn't that kind of girl
just a heartbreak kid looking for a big love story
with her body

a day in the life

petsitting at the deans was the best. you could stay out all night and your folks never knew. i met dana at The Bodyshop. he convinced me to enter the dance competition. i remember how tanned i was in my strapless velour dress with slits up the sides and being pretty happy placing third considering i was the only one left with clothes on. dana smashed the cab door on my leg that night, jealous of this other jerk, a real ladies' man. i slept with dana in the Granville Hotel, could not understand why he never came onto me. didn't know he mainlined shouts outside, some woman, "fuck you cocksucker." i stepped on a large cockroach in bare feet. a fresh scar on dana's chin. didn't seem like much of a fighter. i took off at four a.m. played "Evergreen" by heart in the dark on the piano. danced to "Why don't we do it in the road?" on the deans' lawn by myself. their german shepherd ate their son's gerbil. i bought him a hamster 'cause the store didn't have any gerbils

make that last bus

it's pissin' out 'n i miss the last bus transfer to Phibb's
Exchange. i'm huffin' it up Robson. this guy appears
outside the Sheraton Landmark. asks me why i'm cry
ing. i tell him i missed my bus and i'll be in a ship loada'
trouble if i don't get home. he says he'll give me a ride
he looks okay. looks like her. i'm in love with her so
i've got everybody that slightly resembles her way up
there on a pedestal. he has to run up to his hotel room
and grab his keys. "c'mon" he says. i follow. inside his
hotel room. he asks me what i'll give him. "what do you
mean?" i ask. "a quick fuck for the ride" he says. i tell
him "i'm catholic. i teach catechism. i don't even have
a boyfriend. i can't get pregnant." his head. my mouth
i'd done this before when i was twelve. at least i'd get
home soon. make that last bus. mom and dad would be
relieved.

a/broad

pants undone. a man exits a hotel room in 'La Zapote' where i stay
another room down the hall, a woman leaves her room as i mine. tell
her her blouse is unbuttoned. she looks at me. laughs. the money i have
locked up in the hotel safe is stolen. penniless. stomach squawking. i
price bananas and oranges. two nurses from St.Paul's Hospital. invite

me to stay with them. one is cute. after two days. they leave to tour with
Paco. their friend who believes they have aids. wish i. they wipe out my
meagre fund before leaving. our tour guide has room (a room) for me. (ah
oh.) back. in the hills. walk back blocks off the main drag. road. dusty.
starving dogs. fat dark woman sells tacos on st. corner. stands i've been

warned against. we eat. his house attached to a lumber mill. big bag
of pot. keeps me happy. only one bed. "where will i?" "what do you
think you're here for? i feed and house you. a man needs his daily quota
you owe me something" shoves me onto the bed. pounces. grabs
my arms. i punch back. then bolt. lock myself in the bathroom. bashes

the door down. drags me back to bed. roll and back. scratch him with
stubby nails. grappling. slaps me. pull his hair. pinned. under his grip.
rips off my pants. hard. hammering. the old springs. "i'll be home
tomorrow. i'll be home tomorrow."

to out from under

i.

this is where you meet me

when i'm silent, i crack
when i speak, i crack

                              i can sing high
                         and i can sing low
                    but i crack in the middle

the body knows what the mind doesn't

                              to move forward

              return to the past

maybe if we got stoned enough
she'd let me kiss her   like one time when we were doing crack
and i inhaled a huge rock then stumbled

she caught and held me
for the first time my heart
pounding into her chest. the
rise and fall of her breast against my cheek
where i'd wanted to be   all   those   years

stop doing the things you love to heal from them
been twelve years today   since my last line
                              this eye   ready for weeping

ii.

i can sing high
and i can sing low
but i crack in the middle

find 'em, feed 'em, fuck 'em and forget 'em

i see blue baby in the toilet
pieces of her   refuse
refuse to be flushed
i hammer at the handle
push at the pieces

                        "go away blue baby
                          leave me alone!"

and the one i miscarried at the puget sound guitar camp
i-who-could-not-be-mother
mine the bigger job

                              no longer intent on bodily harm

        capable of goodness
                        (i want to be good, not nice)

the how i am becoming my mother

                        (that ol' rug covers up a lot of sins)

iii.

this singing through of my life
                              where i listen from

you do have to die before you live   *not* shadows rise lazurian

been sober for longer than i've been drunk
put two of them in the clinker (look how far i won't go)

iv.

can you feel my heart behind your eyes fraulein?
remember my first night on your couch
how you covered me with a blanket just a little too short
kissed me deeply and i cried myself to sleep
big old happy tears

many a tear has to fall
but it's all
in the game

i can sing high
and i can sing low

                    without cracking

home and the closeness of the beloved
the place of one's earliest affection
daphne marlatt

you sell the 'old house'

i drive up Adderly the last night i will sleep there   same corner, same bed
sal's favorite song 'always and forever' from highschool on the radio

percy the dog died last week
like he knew
                    he didn't have a new beginning in him

 the for sale sign on the lawn
screaming   SOLD   SOLD
i lay my head on the steering wheel
                                    tears trickle   tickle jowels

        cry inasmuch as narrative requires it

one day at a time
                    sweet jesus

this is not an erotic poem

you are eighteen. i am twenty-nine. you have a baby named poppy and a boyfriend. have never been with a woman. nor have i. chuck set us up. your boyfriend. chuck's boy-toy.

dark liquid eyes. thick lashes. long hair. round breasted. a total femme. nails. we spend hours pushing poppy in the buggy around Stanley Park. talking. the chi climbing up

and over. enveloping the two of us. out for dinner. candlelight. later in my boat bedroom. poppy swathed in blankets under the window. laying down on my bed. whole house

turning. hot and tentative. leaning in and over you. into a place that could be home. this is not an erotic poem. on one elbow. hair falling. across your face.

massaging your scalp. brush your cheek and forehead under my thumb and fingers. this wanting. heart pound swallowing my whole head.

desire larger than the world. honey wild lips. my tongue. flesh of our. mouths meet. electric spill. slip. fall. rise. my thigh between yours

noses touch. little birdbeats between hearts. a wild splashy willing welling. beyond line of. a holding on. holding each other. warm breath clouds over my ear.

beat of one thousand wings. your tongue kiss. long long. stop only to inhale. laugh. slide on top of you. lip-locked. torch-lit. burning.

fire is

it's a bad night for fires. your stomach heavy. his
clumping around in chains. floating upstairs. bonk
of shoes on floor. you the xanthin leaf. wait simple
maple death. downstairs now.

she's dreaming they're in the camps, they already took him
there's fire in your dreams. suicidal vaulting
from the mint-green roof of the Hotel Vancouver, fire
rising weightless between The Canucks and Hollywood Squares

the virgin and Kwan Yin. five smiles cracked
at the right moment. the right angle
grandfather's hand on the arm of the eldest
smell of snow. lilies baptizing the air where

you go a-mothering. quiet rolls off you. and heat
your face. fire is. shouting at you. seen you in Queer
Chroma. on the red side of brightness. red in face.
on fire

s(talking). glance from the vestibule. cornered. moves in for the kill.
prurient thoughts. spring. you stand there like furniture
immeubles. immovable. writing on fire. proverbial pervert.
you are heartily sorry

for having offended. green as prayer
and loud. thrown in fire. burning-happy
as a salamander. to a crisp.
put your eyes together. put your ears together

can't belong to yourself. miswired. misfired. silence of
the accused you. baptismal heir. godmother. flying around
on your burning ironing board. he daydreams about a life
without you

but-the-poem-woke-me-up

welcome everyone to the-middle-of-the-night-notes
the bad-girl-good-girl-wish-my-poems-were-funny-notes
i'm ready for battle   eyeblinds earplugs   wrist braces   mouthguard
everybody's dreamwoman

the gods bellow 'a poet with a Martha Stewart mortgage
is like a mariness with a dead sea-bird around her neck'
just 'cause the v.s.b.'s paid you too little for eight years
don't mean you're gettin' any money honey

i refuse to listen   a quill poking my cheek
cat-hair build-up on the sheets force myself to sleep
o god   the reading is still two nights away   i'm chuggin'
my harmonica in front of the crowd and someone laughs

cat-stretch and whine   he'd love a nocturnal romp
sitting up   staring   ready to continue   what i'm obviously into
how many times can a girl switch the light off and on feign sleep or the desire
to the committee singin' Johnny Nash's *i can see clearly now*

so this is the lucrative writerly hour Shani warned me about
four-thirty a.m. and ready-to-rock-lava-java-lip-hip-let-her-rip-and-roll,
anxious-girl sick-to-stomach-body-shakin'-head-bangin'-allergy-itchin'-
good-bad-blues-a-type-A-not-a-sleep-in-the-day-kind-o'-girl

the staff'd be arriving at Delaney's right about now
almost time for my neighbours to start clang-bangin' downstairs
i could put on my macs and be the first one to English Bay
(how soft is the music this morning and how sweet)

push the jealousy of my poetry prize-winning classmates away
warm palm on cold nose under covers
could get up and start my do-it-yourself-will
instead   i dream a greasy spoon

breaky with bacon and eggs   i'm all achin' and beggs
                                               goodnight

writedowntheline

i still love

she could head into her life with the same ferocity as anyone

i drag you with me

never give up on you
a private people   *mum's the word*

and on that day which we are all standing in

skinless
you find mad grief in my words

"your mother can not speak to you"

the feral daughter "o my god i am heartily sorry…"

receives her penance

you ask me to leave your home

the telephone:

"remember i still love you and wish you well"

we want to love

there is no simple love

i.

at some point one must get on with this business of love

the way love finds us in our bodies
the way love doesn't find us
the way love finds us and we don't see her

love chooses you

ii.

hang out for a while in your body

                                   (i can't breathe
                                   when you hold me tight)

                                   (you can breathe if you can find air)
this keeping a/part to stay together
this refusing what comes easily

is withdrawal emotion?
                          does catching one's breath hurt?

44

iii.

did i mention
the thing that cannot be mentioned

love is not abuse
        is not eating each other just to survive
        is not eating the pigs who ate the girls

you can not paint over injustice
  (lord willing   and the creek still runs)

iv.

there are those who have looked long into the face of fear

i decided to stop loving you today
not interested in fitting my heart around you

sleeping with myself   tonight
all the pieces of me settling in one room

no   i like it   i like it   it's good.

                                        (joy takes hold)

afterwords

i.   sweet country in which i found my home

      the sound of your hair

      falling over your cheeks

ii.   you'd wake me up

      nights in the middle

      "do you love me?"

      child words

      meant for mother

iii.   memory, my (re)course

      the past / still life

      banking coals in the wood stove

      no light left

iv.   i could (not) have loved you more

             wanting my love as it was

             cabin f(or)ever

v.   honey/suckle me

             open up like your thighs, full

             <occupy the whole> of / words

             slide

             in-between

             my mouth

vi.   and ear

                Eros.

                       Erosion

love or something

envision opening   like a flower   delivery
roses like bone   body-smooth   big white bow

worldwide we deliver fast fresh cuts
unconditional guarantee
24 Hrs say it with flowers 444-4444

there is easy once you have it
you've never received flowers before

surrounded by bounty speeding ahead of the crowd
don't know what you did to deserve this, you
left makeup under your eyes this morning

Catherine,
  thinking of you
       Sherri

is this how love starts smiling?
top row of teeth over bottom lip, you

don't know how to feel, take
maracas, castanets out of Grammo's vase
unwrap cellophane (the receiving blanket)

remove water tubes think
about what you'll say

snip leather leaf, stems   at 110 degrees
inhale each rose like love
while ferns hold baby's breath in a headlock

you drop a penny in the wishing well
fix on the scent, can a girl have too many flowers

warming her house?
your icing-head-candy-tail-cat watches this performance
hollers   pounces   on a reed

your eyes eat the light, eat the green, hear
they come through your dreams, the sun

looks closely, snaps back, you're seeing ghosts
out of the sides of your eyes
four ferrets, two cats and a teenager underground

"Get back on your pedestal!" you liked her
better when you hardly knew her

bill bissett says "there are phonecalls in the air, crackling
in the wires," you dance the pumpnut on your porch, wired
wild radiance spills from the arrangement

you're certain nothing leaves the planet too soon
not the suicide-float-by-dream-thoughts

silences between sounds
sounds between stars
notes between ears

you can admit you don't know who you are
torqued upside-down   bed

when the people rise, rise
when the people bed
can she give her guns to Brinks?

she watches the watch, (Nanny's clock on Spruce)
endless tic, says time is it.

you could get up and make coffee
feel the day's eyes adjust her soft lenses
the cat's rubbing his, you reach to pat

he runs off, he's seen his double
dart naked from toilet to goosedown

at the housewarming last night, you sang the moon up
till 11:05 when someone turned your lights off
waxing coffee in to carpet

what are you doing at forty-one stumbling around in the dark
in a condo you own?

once you asked your guests to leave, your lights
were miraculously restored
on days like these

leaf/drop   treeless
petal-fall   like eyelashes

you're never going to have a wife
if you keep fooling around with her
allowing the slow drip taurus slip bend and point you here, sliding

toward each other
along a trajectory
called love, exchange

fluids tentatively
she's under   your third skin

you can not come to ground
pocket her silence
who sets this madding pace? your heart   full

aches in your hand, turns leathery
finally there's not all that much

you can say, the fullmoon has you so turned on
giant green peppers, sweet potatoes, dance half-human,

writhing heads of buddhist deities float in dream-river around
your dad's farm you whisk them from the water, decapitate them
en theos, sustenance for months

wash all dust from your writing body
listen to her feet talk   invite the incomparable Sappho

to Arcadia

to sip under an olive tree
heed your   *equations*
of love

fugue

romance wants to be

on a Saturday morning

                forced to follow the pull of the line

                         pull the lid off

there she drops

                  weightless   between page and i

        brushing my   (breaking) my   body/heart

have i known enough loneliness

        live in a small place

        avoid my own goodness

dream: lacusta lacuna drives us to Lesbos (loves her too)

        shows us his dress shoe from the front seat

                         olive trees stalk exhausted hills

        am i but half a tree?

scene of her

    shock of her

            hair

by the window

                   all the words she didn't say

         i overheard

             understood

the roof caved in today

above the doorway

         excavare, f. cavus, cave

hollow

shallow

hallowed be thy

          breath

                  remembering / my forgetting

suite from the hot tub

i.

she'll never forget me

she'll take me to Germany

and i will be Canada

                    how easily i give up

                                        everything for nothing

rising

                falling
                            on my belly

            lapryoscopic scars

                                        freckles

this book of mine

ii.

apnea.

    how not to chuck
        this text into the arms of the enemy

goosepimples
      nipples slow buds of desire manifold

all things uttered censored made equal

listen to her breath

 loosed upon the closed bodyheart
        chiming still as earth air

the ocean, my ear

        her downy skin
        eyes, a black to sit in
        the sound of starlight

iii.

        all the world turning her away

        the incarnate crying to incarnate

        night of their conception

the flapping-falling-open-ended-broken-down

            beat.   beat of wings

this arm over my belly
    tucked in like clouds

            these words

                  i breathe
                  the page

douce france

the full moon appeared through a peephole
the day they cut out my super blondissima

                                revealing the grey matter

i turned and saw you move your chair close to mine
not to adore you would have been a sin

quelle belle surprise, this *coup de foudre*
how i have missed you all of my life, me

                                in love with nameless things, love
                                falls on my hot heart
                                        like snowflakes

you want to know the colour
what lies behind the eyes;

                            the candles in them:

                                      un coeur d'enfant

my love marks, my aphrodite
the blue on my thigh yellows, you

                                cup my face in your palms, gaze
                                into my eyes, kiss me

something always in one hand :

                        a french dictionary
                        cafe valencia
                        mes pantouffles

you leave my upper lip wet
my face tight at day's end

later we walk in sync
you more beautiful with raindrops in your hair

knots in tree trunks   *les triangles de Venus*
        shadows of fire hydrants   sweet breasts

our shadows on the sidewalk, a photograph in black and white
my mother and her father on Hastings

                                in dress coats, arm in arm

in bed the wind rhapsodizes at regular intervals
there is as much safety in your breathing out
                                as when my father snored

i watch your sleeping face
the halfmoons of your lips
                        wax

and i wonder

                how i finally got here

58

mutual notes

i.

maples and mo(u)rning
the colour of sweetgrass burning

she is born   out of time   against her
has not eaten for days
                              perhaps weeks

does not look up when i call her name

bodyswagger   to water
                              head bobs   tongue laps
                                                       in'n out in'n out

how many laps left?

ii.

O Bonny Jean

she settles beside the writers fest program
antennae ears on Isabelle Allende's insight
                                        into her next chapter
the table's stain/her browns

i bring her chicken in broth baby food
wretches at the smell
                    medical reduced protein
                    on her fur
                              (coats the first to go)

as i load up the syringe
                    i am in grammo's kitchen
cats on the counter picking

still
        the heart murmurs

iii.

feel each bone of your spine
                                        under my fingers
cradle your cheek
                        my palm
run my nose up fur\head
'tween ears and speckled whiskertickle

    i kiss   kiss
invent links between human and animal

love   i lavish love

how many kisses can send you to all my relations
to that goodnight

                            but then things of this world
                                    hold little interest
for us now

iv.

she lives in a small place
                        a basket a closet

(think about the quality of her life)

she knows waiting
                        facing the wail
is almost used to herself

she knows the way to mother
wishes she was before all this

v.

dying this dying
patiently the sphinx

we three   this holy table
do not play Mozart,   Matthew Good
the register foreign

vi.

feeble cries in my ambulance
license plate beside reads 'Ave'
and I wonder if i've said enough

her cries

                (just make her comfortable,
                like you would with people)

haibun #2, where you meet me

she smells like spirits out from the grass, is lint on an adverse
road fleeing from the crazy woman, a dustbuster grafted onto
her arm, she's broken the pheromone spell, eaten a lb. of dirt
behind the plastic wall where day breaks all over the undrunk,
while squirrels are flying across Barclay st. on chestnut boughs,
civilization encroaches on black brants, Palestine is the rage of
the dying, *this is where you meet me.* gram's skull could come
up and drive me away, on this familiar afternoon, illness impales
my tumescent hollow arms. it isn't all sugar plum dreams, muscle-
gargoyled, wasting, a bird body, bur/de(n), the bloody body chronic
grumbling under stomach, waits for you to raise them, ghostdancers,
in the November sky, weep all over the tiny rooves, star-struck vine
maples chase one another, baring their teeth cross my heart, hope
to die underground, the old house makes a wish, her pretty eyes and
half conversations on stilts between us. friends around me buy stocks
and bonds, their nails hooked under their incisors, undertongue, their
tea cups rock, they hear light under the door, light cracking from keep-
ing up with the Jones, under their shirts rosaries not said for decades,
my skin holds small memories, cant this: mothers remember to mother
and the heart, remember to protect her, bundle your medicine, forget
who i slept with last night (i have), eros is locked in her tower, sits in
the blue sun, clothed in small songs.

neilology

(for Al Neil, deep cove jazz musician)

Dollarton beachside squatters colony. waiting for Lowry. the North Shore
mud flat counter culture. Cates Park. three hundred year old cedar giants.
spines press up & down. plum deeper *molecular compositions*. wind-
shrieks. atonal free forms. warped windows. drizzle on Burrard
Inlet. granitic hills. snare-drum pebbles. arms awash in rain & roots. a
crepuscular fog of half-stifled e-motion. lilypad croakings. like a cheap
radio picking up two stations at once. homing into a slow drag tempo
napalm bomb gimmick. throwing down something new from Art Pepper's
junk dream. center has to hold. point where the stuff's flying out from. *my
mother is so fuckin' high, she had to wear dark glasses to avoid the White Light.*
open the suture on top of your head. shoot the energy right where
you need it. pop the p's. whippersnapper. beboparoonie. pause in your
straight-ahead life. still the appetite for war. mass-acceptable dog-eat
dogma. insomniac's nightmare. bow constrictions. empty bottles of
Caravel Ruby Red. whip her snapper. i might even rape you. ex-con.
ride 'em cowboy. counterpoint. bluebird whistles. klangfarben.
all pitches sound around the note. the room. the people. pop 'em.
keeper of the avant-garde flame. grunts. gamboling & gambling of
hands. rummaging inside the piano. groans. blurred fury of motion.
vertiginous pseudo-downbeat. downboy. deep cove homeboy. angry
lobsters. hither. zither. squeaks. trash & carry mod-pop time of any
thing goes. global aural would-be collage. facility & abandon. little
dinky pinky over elephant keys. mutate standards. fuck tradition. rattle
off ninths 'n tenths. *if you want to play like Bird, you have to live like*

Bird. eeks. dip so maniacally. jugs of Calona Red. first job. thirteen
years old. delivering condoms to hookers. wrestling ghosts from the
strings with *blue voodoo glue*. not-just-for-the-hell-of-it. apocalyptic.
cat tap out of tune arpeggios on the battered upright. *keep the porn bits
in*. the piano a woman's body. non-existence of time in music. as the
heart beats. fill in the clear crystals. *seek a way out of darkness*. who
needs an audience when you're playing to the creator. Lowry's coming
with a boot-legged bottle. *giving me all this for killing the germans*.
crawling. on all fours down Dollarton Highway. into the arms of the
North Shore Bulls.

a walking song

Granville, Howe, Hornby, Burrard, Thurlowe, Bute, Jervis, Nicola, Broughton
Cardero, Bidwell, Denman, Chilco, Lagoon Drive, Stanley Park. illusion that
nothing's there. bruising myself against car fumes and your second hand
smoke. clapping down image. wedging into bodyland.

Rosemary Brown crosses Locarno Beach. eagle overhead digests heron
eggs. & the geometry of camera men. Rose wading out to sea in pink, short
sleeved blouse, cream shorts, Burks in left hand, a man's white straw hat
on her head. rocks in pockets.

cultural practice in this crabbed wilderness of mandatory clothing & trouble-
somely streets that tear holes in the monastery and rip off the figs strapped
to the body. July stirs up things. blue flowers in the blood. like this tide com-
ing in. unobtrusive. how she comes up behind god's back.

Rose rocking on a log. we want some fairy familiars. family stories. Maya.
hold the balance cart. i'll put you in Jeff's shadow. o.k. now we can do some
footage in your garden.

sweet artifice of consciousness. smell isn't everything. she carries me around
the block and the gazebo. behind Barclay Manor. warning: these premises are
protected by video surveillance.

what you trippin' on? can you see my underwear? put me down. don't say bye to me. screw hippy. mandolins quiver inside my legs. my rhetoric hung over. the way Barclay and Nicola jeer at me.

all around me bees sharpen their feet. up stairs. Polaris stretches. eyelids covered with night. bespeckled spectacle meant for whom? switch some invisible street lights on. i shall not eat my evening.

o don't tell them i'm looking down over the imagined. coquette. that i stitch poems into the crown of my hat. that i'm paranoid & popping in for a pee. o don't tell 'em.

contrapuntal listening

i hear the leaves on the hibiscus. they're soon to be demolished
cuz' i was born with one eye and make a pass at the moon every
chance i get. i own her. i swallow her to decode my own hand.

i look for things underfoot like Kiyooka in his kodakcolapostcards.
don't ask me why. i told the truth about my first/last drunk occurring
as a possibility. of the death of the mother in me. ain't. woman who
can't get over this thing of confluences. the invisible is coming.

objects are closer than they appear. butterboycatsmell of turnips at
mom & dad's on sunday. ladeedadeeda. is this inheriting the earth.
my deadcat rebukes me. the sky looks worried. hasn't the ministry
prepared us? i'm giving up the ghost hoping my insides are in the
rightplace as i'm sitting sideways. in myself.

endometrial ablation insufficient. "we can leave the bottom bit of
your cervix in." hyster-wrecked me. i've come undone. i've lost the
sun. guess who? heart outside my skin. St. Paul's patient-drop-off.
in-the-out-door.

a walk-in never taking a breath. early morn' of seagulls wings &
fractal sealight. bebop to pitterpantherpatter by the duke. dream all
day long. shall i see my captain as i cross the bar? people wanting to
leave so soon while Dr. Van Belzin busy storing the organs of dead
children.

& everyone on psychotropics. seagull squall. body sleeps in second
position. corn moon between my legs. fecal matter from waterfowl
leeching into Georgia Strait and i don't recognise my hands. we're all
canaries in the mine dying. mere throw aways. if i could buy silence.
in the west end. clamber out of the well worn dip in my mattress.

this work through which my whole life sings. may i have your eyes?
listen to Chopin's Melissma with your ear while fluid jingles my anvil.
taste the beast within your beauty for each day my alien grows 600%

as the bus coughs i forget my narrative. as things underfoot are less
reliable. as objects loom larger than & not what they appear. as my
eye askew, iris-blue, pupil-white, as the other, pupil-blue,iris-white
as one is in the chimney, as the other in the pot.

an old load, an old year. i'll never hear a mother ship rumble in
forgotten places. we could flatstone up the lazy river. open on the
cottage of the thin past while the cat's ears grey and i think about
dyeing his fur. cover my head. evanesce.

upon a time once

up on her sleepy ears a dreamvoice niagarously roars
"wake up and listen to your mother!"
oh my, half-baked thoughts   that's a kickstart

she has been in the corner of a drawer for some weeks
dragging (herself) on in the privacy of herself
the green fool

she cannot help how she looks
from squeezing her skin each night
i could die she thinks   then i'd be rid of it

now she goes to the wall everyday with her cut-outs   her bag of
words under the words
tips her head back

sips her coffee sees the sky   blue blind   sunstripped
puts on her shades, a penny stuck to the right lens, she
has too many mornings, a thousand miles to go

in the BarNone Café, Courtenay
she clunks around with her chains on
beside her a man   holes in his sweater darned

catpulls in his dirty-blue terry-towel cap
she wonders what the cottonwood might say
given what the cottonwood sees if he fell over dead-drunk

caught daydreaming her way into a poem
when she was a girl, she liked everything going
now her feet on the ground   she feels an undercurrent

not sure if she's here or not
she knows she isn't there, she's somewhere
really can't remember   she's many places at once

trusts the driver ahead of her
wants to hide in the city

the hordes that stream past her at five
warm her   she is all
hammered by them

the wind is her enemy
one false move   her paper bits can vanish
into the ropy air, a blatant act of resistance

in her dream she was punished for recording her family history

she sings
notes that haven't been
their high laughter   new in her mouth
a grace-note

follows her nose   eye in her stomach
a bad-fantasy-head-dream-girl nibbles at her psyche, she
carries her around for a day or two, has felt

this freight for some years
she likes her heartlogic
thinks there's nothing the matter with her

if she could just get on with a little light fluff
at the end of the day
climb into the trees

on the *heron priested shore*
stay
for ever   and ever

amen.

acknowledgements

and thanks ...

i am profoundly indebted to betsy warland, my mentor, to shauna paull, editor extraordinaire and the entire milieu collective, and to my teachers : my aunt florence mcneil, bill bissett, george mcwhirter, lorna crozier, daphne marlatt, nicole brossard, lisa robertson, meredith quartermain, and dionne brand, as well as the many other astounding writers that have been my teachers and support.

i have infinite gratitude to craig, my twin, jane and colleen, my sisters, and janit bianic, my sensitive first reader.

i thank my publisher, c.a. casey, of gusgus press, for seeing the value in this work and guiding me through it in a helpful and meaningful manner, and my friend lori kenney, for her cover art. thank you also to the many friends who have tirelessly attended my reading and concerts. you know who you are.

some of these poems were previously published in :

sappho's corner poetry series vol. 5
exact fare only 2
the fed anthology
love poems for the media age
oval victory
all wound up
coastlines iv
chasing haley's comet
a writer's world
crabs
room
quills
sinister wisdom
one cool word
chroma
west coast line
the capilano review
rampike
event
roots
whetstone

Credit for quotes

"papa was a rollin stone," by the Temptations, writers: N. Whitfield and B. Strong 1972

"to out from under"
D. Riley, "Dry Air"
words Carl Sigman, music Gen. C. G. Dawes, "It's All In The Game"

"suite from the hot tub"
B. Warland, "Breathing the Page"

"thirsty"
D. Marlatt, "Seven Glass Bowls"
"i still love," D. Brand

"we want to love"
L. Robertson, "Debbie an Epic"
D. Brand, "thirsty"
B. Warland, "What Holds Us Here" last 3 quotes
Words and music by Elton John and B. Taupin, "Someone saved my life tonight"

"love or something"
S. Thesen, "The Pangs of Sunday"

"you sell the 'old house'"
D. Marlatt, "Seven Glass Bowls"
L. Robertson, "the weather"
D. Brand, "thirsty"
B. Warland, "What Holds Us Here"

"neilology"
al neil, autobiographical collages, 1980's

"upon a time once,"
D. Thomas, "Poem in October"

cat mac, singer-songwriter from Vancouver, BC, is the recipient of Milieu's Emerging Writer's Contest for her first collection of poetry *under the influence*. She has poems from her new manuscript *Emily and Elspeth* in *Queer Chroma* (England), *Rampike*, and *Sinister Wisdom*. Publications include *Event, The Capilano Review,* and *West Coast Review*, anthologies include *Exact Fare 2* and *The Fed Anthology* (Arsenal).